Crises of Governments

Crises of Governments

The Ongoing Global Financial Crisis
and Recession

ROBERT BARRO

The Institute of Economic Affairs

First published in Great Britain in 2011 by
The Institute of Economic Affairs
2 Lord North Street
Westminster
London SW1P 3LB
in association with Profile Books Ltd

The mission of the Institute of Economic Affairs is to improve public understanding of the fundamental institutions of a free society, with particular reference to the role of markets in solving economic and social problems.

A CIP catalogue record for this book is available from the British Library.

ISBN 978 0 255 36657 1

Many IEA publications are translated into languages other than English or are reprinted. Permission to translate or to reprint should be sought from the Director General at the address above.

Typeset in Stone by MacGuru Ltd
info@macguru.org.uk

Printed and bound in Britain by Hobbs the Printers

CONTENTS

THE AUTHOR

Robert Barro is the Paul M. Warburg Professor of Economics at Harvard University; a Senior Fellow of the Hoover Institution of Stanford University; and a Research Associate of the National Bureau of Economic Research. He has a PhD in Economics from Harvard University and a BS in Physics from Caltech. Robert Barro is also co-editor of Harvard's quarterly *Journal of Economics* and was recently president of the Western Economic Association and vice-president of the American Economic Association. His academic research has included research into macroeconomics and economic growth, focusing on the empirical determinants of economic growth, the economic effects of public debt and budget deficits, and the formation of monetary policy. His current research focuses on two very different topics: the interplay between religion and political economy and the impact of rare disasters on asset markets.

FOREWORD

The IEA was delighted that Professor Robert Barro agreed to give the 2011 Hayek Memorial Lecture. As will be clear from reading his lecture, Professor Barro has an impressive record of research into aspects of economics that are particularly relevant at the current time. Perhaps of particular relevance is his work on fiscal policy. In the wake of the financial crisis, many countries undertook significant fiscal expansions to try to create jobs and increase economic growth. Other countries – including the UK – have since announced programmes of fiscal consolidation. It will be some time before it is possible to obtain robust data that indicate whether so-called fiscal expansions increased economic growth, but the preliminary evidence certainly accords with the picture painted by Professor Barro in the Hayek lecture. The increases in government borrowing led to some very short-term growth but this was followed by significant reductions in growth. This is consistent with the long-term fiscal multiplier being negative. Why should this be so? Again, Professor Barro's work points the way to the answer. In the first place, government borrowing has to be funded – which itself affects the economy – and, in addition, taxes eventually have to be raised to pay down the debt or, at least, to reverse the increase in government borrowing. Growth will fall when those extra taxes are levied or, possibly, before they are levied if households anticipate them.

It is interesting too how such a process affects the policy debate – a debate that is well under way in the UK. When growth reverses after the very short-term effects of the fiscal stimulus wear off, proponents of fiscal stimulus packages respond by arguing that the packages were insufficient. They do not appreciate that a medium-term reversal of growth is the likely result of the earlier stimulus.

Professor Barro's warnings about particular aspects of fiscal stimulus packages are also prescient. For example, the recent extension of unemployment benefits in the USA has led to increased unemployment and increased unemployment terms.

Although F. A. Hayek and Professor Barro would agree on the dangers of a so-called fiscal expansion led by increased government spending in times of recession, Professor Barro is not an Austrian-school economist. In the Hayek lecture he argued in favour of the rescue of financial institutions at the time of the financial crisis. At the same time, however, he does worry about how the process of quantitative easing is going to be managed.

In his analysis of the financial crisis Professor Barro blames, to a large extent, the increase in securitisation and suggests that the government agencies that promoted this phenomenon should be privatised. He also suggests, however, that we have, more or less, learned the lessons from the recent financial crash and the particular combination of mistakes that led to that crash is unlikely to happen again.

Nevertheless, in Professor Barro's view, that does not mean that we can be sanguine about the economic outlook. The lecture ends with compelling evidence that the next economic crisis will be caused by government indebtedness. This crisis will arise because of both the explicit and implicit government debt that has been built up within the EU and within US states. The lecture ends with a discussion of possible ways to avert such a crisis.

This lecture can be commended for its important contribution to economic thinking on the recent financial crisis and its aftermath, as well for its incisive and clearly expressed analysis of looming economic problems in the Western world.

PHILIP BOOTH

Editorial and Programme Director,
Institute of Economic Affairs
Professor of Insurance and Risk Management,
Cass Business School, City University

September 2011

The views expressed in this monograph are, as in all IEA publications, those of the author and not those of the Institute (which has no corporate view), its managing trustees, Academic Advisory Council members or senior staff.

ACKNOWLEDGEMENTS

The Institute of Economic Affairs would like to thank CQS for its very generous sponsorship of the 2011 Hayek Memorial Lecture and of this publication.

SUMMARY

- The 'Great Recession' has been particularly deep. In the USA, the loss of GDP relative to trend growth has been 9 per cent. The recovery from recession has also been much slower than the recovery from the recessions of the early 1980s and early 1990s. After those recessions, the USA achieved economic growth of 4.3 per cent and 3.6 per cent respectively.
- The slump has not been nearly as bad as the US Great Depression, though the fall in stock market values of over 50 per cent was the second-largest in history. This compares with a fall in the stock market of 79 per cent during the Great Depression. Furthermore, house prices have fallen by 37 per cent since the financial crash.
- One of the major causes of the crash was the boom in securitisation whereby inherently risky loans were packaged together and sold as very low-risk securities. This was strongly encouraged by the government; Fannie Mae and Freddie Mac, the government agencies responsible, should be privatised.
- The US government was right to bail out the systemically risky banks. However, other aspects of the fiscal stimulus package were misguided for various reasons.
- In general a fiscal stimulus package might raise output in the very short run but the long-term fiscal multiplier is negative.

This leads growth to stall after an initial increase, as is happening at the moment.

- If fiscal stimulus packages are to be used at all then they should be based around reducing taxes so that the tax reductions stimulate work, investment and enterprise. While some of the spending increases have just been a waste of money, others have been very damaging. For example, the significant lengthening of the duration of unemployment payments has caused a rise in the unemployment rate of between 1 and 2 per cent.
- Spending and welfare programme entitlements grew rapidly under President George W. Bush and that growth has continued under President Obama. In many respects, as far as economic policy is concerned, Bush and Obama are 'twins', just as Reagan and Clinton were 'twins'.
- There should be concerns about the exit strategy from the process of quantitative easing. It will be difficult for central banks to avoid both inflation and recession.
- The next crisis will be a crisis of government debt. This debt consists of both explicit borrowing and also of entitlements through social security programmes that have been dramatically expanded under Presidents Bush and Obama. This crisis of government debt is not just a US problem.
- The coming crisis can be addressed in the USA only by reforming entitlement programmes and also by tax reform to reduce 'tax expenditures' or special exemptions from taxes for certain types of economic activity. In the EU, fiscal and monetary policy need to be decoupled so that member states do not become responsible for each other's borrowing.

FIGURES AND TABLES

Crises of Governments

1 CRISES OF GOVERNMENTS: THE ONGOING GLOBAL FINANCIAL CRISIS AND RECESSION

Introduction

It is a great pleasure to be here. I certainly could not resist giving a lecture that is named after Hayek, not to mention following in the footsteps of my great friend Gary Becker, who I believe delivered the lecture last year.

I will talk about the recession, financial crisis and, as mentioned, about the government responses in terms of fiscal stimulus packages and other matters. As a brief introduction, I think the central origin of the crisis, particularly in the United States, was from the housing market, and I will try to detail why I think that is true. An important part of the cause was the problems caused in the housing markets by mortgage financing and the developments in that sector. I think there was a critical mistake made in terms of underestimating the possibility that housing prices could fall on average because this was an unprecedented event, particularly in terms of the magnitude of the decline in average house prices that occurred. I think that was the precipitating agent for the crisis, both in the USA and elsewhere. And indeed, this aspect of house prices interacted with developments in the financial sector, in terms of new products, securitisations, and so on.

I think a number of mistakes were made here, but I think that it is critical to realise that the lessons from these mistakes have basically been learned, particularly by the financial sector, and it is unlikely that the next crisis is going to look similar to the last crisis. As such, it is not the best source of policy change to try to fix the mistake that caused the last crisis from which the main lessons have already been learned. I think the most likely next crisis is going to have to do with governments per se.

The recession and recovery in context

So let me try to give some of the data. This will be from a US perspective but I think a lot of it is global in nature. Figure 1 illustrates the course of the Great Recession from the US perspective measured in terms of the growth rate of the real gross domestic product. I think you can see readily the recession, in terms of the negative part. This recession accumulates to a decline in GDP by 4.1 per cent. I don't know if that sounds impressive, but it is actually the largest post-Second World War decline in GDP. It is bigger than the other recessions since the war, not by a lot, but a little bit bigger. It certainly does not measure up to the Great Depression of the 1930s. In this metric it is not at all comparable.

If you look at GDP relative to trend then you can say there was a loss of 9 per cent in GDP, which makes the recession look bigger, because the US economy normally grows at about 3 per cent per year. If instead of that we have negative 4.1 per cent for some period, that is a substantial loss relative to normal growth.

The other thing that has been true, and has been particularly of concern recently, is the weakness of the recovery period, which is shown in Figure 1. The average growth rate of GDP since the recovery began is less than 3 per cent per year, which means that it

Figure 1   **GDP growth since 2000 (annualised)**

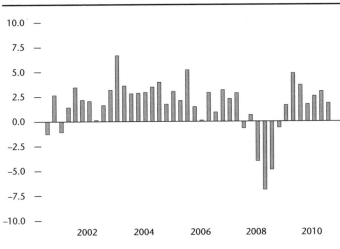

is not really a recovery in the sense of restoring total output back to
the trend. This, I think, relates to why the labour market has been
so weak. So it has been a very disappointing recovery and in fact
it looks worse now than it did perhaps six months ago or so. By
way of contrast, you can look at recoveries from some other recessions. One is the Reagan period, basically the 1980s. Here there is
a pretty substantial recession through 1982, but then the recovery
is quite remarkable (see Figure 2). For pretty much the rest of the
1980s going into 1990 the average growth rate in the recovery
period is 4.3 per cent per year, and I think a lot of this particular
recovery is driven by tax policy changes. There were quite substantial reductions in marginal income tax rates in this period – the
early 1980s and again in 1986. This was something new, really,
that Reagan had led, and I think it was quite an important factor

Figure 2   'Reagan recovery' after the 1982 recession (annualised growth)

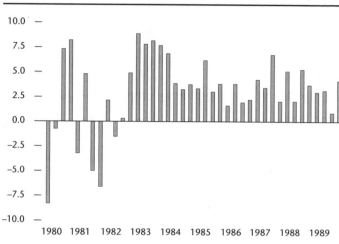

in terms of the strength of the recovery. So an average growth rate well over 4.4 per cent for a long period is something impressive and very different from the current recovery.

Another period you can look at is the 1990s. This is another strong period in the USA and is mostly when Clinton was president. This follows the moderate recession around 1991. The average growth rate in this recovery is a little bit lower than Reagan, it is 3.6 per cent per year, but it is a very extended recovery – basically almost all the 1990s going into 2000. The two heroes in terms of post-Second World War economic policy and results in the USA, I think, are Reagan and Clinton, which shows you how non-partisan I am in my approach to results! I think that, at least in the way things turned out, Clinton was quite a conservative in terms of economic policy, and I think in that sense he is

Figure 3 'Clinton recovery' after the 1990 recession (annualised growth)

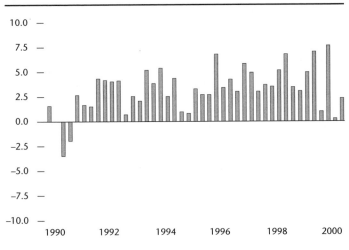

kind of a twin with Reagan rather than being something different from him.

Table 1 shows the global nature of the Great Recession. The US decline that I have mentioned was a little more than 4 per cent going up to the end of the recession in early 2009. The USA is certainly not exceptional in terms of the severity of the recession it experienced – it is actually a little bit less than the average. For these 21 OECD countries the extent of the GDP decline averages about 5.5 per cent, somewhat more than the USA. Several countries have declines of more than 10 per cent, which is the metric I usually use to determine whether or not a rare macroeconomic disaster has occurred. Some countries, such as Japan and Ireland and Finland, are in that category: the decline in those countries was more than 10 per cent. Greece would be in that category if you included the whole of 2010, which is not included in this table. So we can see that several countries have suffered declines in GDP of more than 10 per cent.

Table 1 **The Great Recession in 21 OECD countries**

Country	Peak quarter	Trough quarter	Cumulative decline
Australia	2008.3	2008.4	1.0
Austria	2008.2	2009.2	5.1
Belgium	2008.2	2009.1	4.3
Canada	2008.3	2009.2	3.3
Denmark	2007.4	2009.2	7.9
Finland	2008.2	2009.2	10.2
France	2008.1	2009.1	3.9
Germany	2008.1	2009.1	6.6
Greece	2008.2	2009.1	3.5
Ireland	2007.4	2009.4	14.3
Italy	2008.1	2009.2	7.0
Japan	2008.1	2009.1	10.0
Netherlands	2008.1	2009.2	5.3
New Zealand	2007.4	2009.1	2.4
Norway	2007.4	2009.2	2.5
Portugal	2008.2	2009.1	3.6
Spain	2008.1	2009.4	4.9
Sweden	2007.4	2009.1	7.6
Switzerland	2008.2	2009.2	3.2
United Kingdom	2008.1	2009.3	6.4
United States	2007.4	2009.2	4.1
Simple average	2008.1	2009.2	5.6

Another indicator of the events is the information we can obtain from financial markets, specifically information from the US stock market. Figure 4 shows the pattern of long-term returns from the US stock market. You can pick out the periods of major booms in the stock market and major collapses. And this was particularly important as a signal of what was going on in the worst of the Great Recession in the USA, which is early 2009. You can see where the bottom is, and it looked very serious if you consider what financial markets were predicting at that point. They were predicting a decline that was much worse than the decline that actually happened in practice. Now, some people just denigrate the stock market as not being a very good forecasting tool, but in fact it is better than almost anything you have available, even though it is certainly imperfect. At that time I wrote a column for the *Wall Street Journal* about the probability of the USA getting into a depression type of scenario, and particularly based the column on the stock market return information. I said that the probability of a depression-type scenario was something like 30 per cent, which is enormously high. I remember talking to a reporter and she said, 'What do you mean, the probability is thirty per cent? Is it going to happen or isn't it?'! I find, at least in the USA, that you can't talk about probabilities when you talk to journalists. Anyway, that's what I thought was true at the time. So this was quite a serious threat, and from that perspective things have not worked out nearly as badly as they might have done.

Figure 4 is just showing periods of major stock market booms and busts over the long term going back to 1913. Table 2 shows that the worst stock market bust is associated with the Great Depression. From 1929 to 1932 there is a decline in real value on the stock market of an amazing 79 per cent. Very little of this is

Figure 4 **Cumulative real total stock return**
Proportionate scale, relative to January 1913

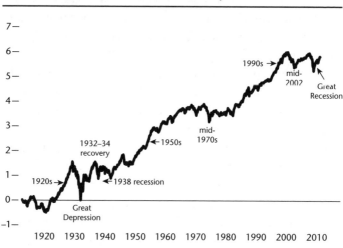

the crash in 1929 itself: it is actually the accumulation over three years that gives you that remarkable reduction. And the recent period is the second-worst decline in the whole of recent history: it is a decline in real value up until the beginning of March 2009 of more than 50 per cent. And I think that was a serious negative signal, and things have rebounded somewhat since then. Nevertheless, we had a serious crisis.

Figure 5 shows us changes in house prices. Again, I think this suggests a major downturn. The figure shows data from the Case-Shiller Price Indices, which are very high-quality measures of house prices. The data represent the real value of average house prices in the United States, and you can see that there is this remarkable period of boom in house prices with average real prices growing by more than 80 per cent in the period from

Table 2 **Major US stock market booms and busts since 1913**

Booms	
Period	Cumulative increase (per cent)
1923.10–1929.08	519
1932.05–1934.01	282
1949.05–1956.03	449
1994.06–2000.08	328
Busts	
Period	Cumulative decrease (per cent)
1929.08–1932.05	79.4
1937.02–1938.03	49.8
1972.12–1974.11	47.4
2000.08–2002.09	47.3
2007.10–2009.02	51.7

1997 to roughly 2006. There are a lot of reasons that have been put forward for this amazing boom, and I will talk about some of the possible factors. But the boom, of course, is followed by this equally amazing bust in house prices: a decline of something like 37 per cent in real terms of average house prices in a period going up to, say, 2009. That really is an unprecedented shock from the standpoint of the US economy. I think it is central that, *ex ante*, financial markets put zero probability weight on this kind of a result in terms of the house price declines, and that underlies a lot of the problems, including those of Lehman Brothers, but also other difficulties in the financial sector. It is also disturbing that there has not been a rebound in house prices of any significance, even up to today. It looked like there was some increase but in

Figure 5 **US real house prices**
Nominal values divided by CPI, 2000.1=100

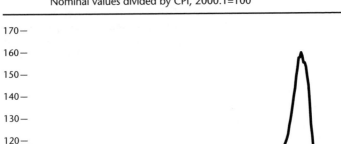

the last months house prices have actually fallen on average by another 7 per cent or so. So there isn't really a rebound that you yet see in this metric.

If we look at commercial real estate prices we find that the accumulated decline associated with the Great Recession in that sector is about the same as the decline in the residential sector (30 per cent to 40 per cent), but the decline clearly occurs later. I think it is a reasonable inference that the problems started in the residential mortgage and housing sector and then spread elsewhere, including to commercial real estate.

Causes of the boom and bust

Part of what is propelling the boom and the bust, I think, is related to developments in securitisation. Figure 6 shows the volume of issue of securities related to residential mortgages. This shows a remarkable volume of issuance of these kinds of securities. In one year, there were $2.4 trillion of mortgage-backed securities issued. We can see that the number of sub-prime and Alt-A mortgages that were securitised grew very rapidly – these were the higher-risk mortgages. So I think a lot of the boom in the housing market had to do with the fact that there was a lot of cheap financing available to people who normally would not have been eligible for mortgages – it is these mortgages that were categorised as 'sub-prime'. This was partly propelled by the government and partly by the reasoning that prevailed in financial markets that somehow you could create risk-free securities by packaging these mortgages up. So there was an incredible volume of sub-prime mortgages being securitised.

There are two amazing inventions here which, if either of them were correct, would have been one of the most remarkable inventions ever. One is the idea that you can take a lot of garbage paper (sub-prime mortgages) but then you package them all together and you somehow diversify it all and then the investment ends up being AAA – or at least the upper tranches of the security end up being AAA. So you could create this vast amount of more or less risk-free paper by putting together a lot of junk. Now, if that were correct that would of course be one of the most brilliant things ever. And people did have confidence in this new device for some period, but it doesn't work too well when the average price of houses falls by 30 per cent to 40 per cent.

Alt-A is also a very interesting invention. You take people who don't normally qualify for mortgages because they cannot document their income, etc. Then you assume that these people

Figure 6   **US residential mortgage-backed securities (RMBS)**
$ billion, 2000 prices

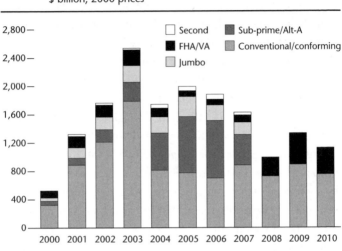

are prime borrowers and so you call them 'Alt-A' and you basically provide mortgage financing on terms that are not too different from prime. That didn't work out too well either. In the end Alt-A did not perform all that differently from sub-prime in terms of defaults. So I think these are two sources of the problems that caused the crash.

The US government has had an amazing amount of involvement with the mortgage sector which has not happened in other countries. The US Congress over many years, working through Fannie Mae and Freddie Mac especially, has particularly tried to expand the mortgage market so that more or less everybody could own their own home. This was done by extending credit to people who did not normally qualify. And the government-sponsored enterprises, Fannie Mae and Freddie Mac, were, to a large extent, the vehicle for this expansion. Of course, the reason why they essentially went bankrupt in September 2008 was because of the sub-prime and Alt-A products that they had amassed on their books. They amassed tremendous amounts of paper which at some point was rated AAA but was in fact really sub-prime and Alt-A. I think the government involvement in the mortgage business in the United States is a crucial part of the picture, and I think going forward that it is important in the USA to phase out the government involvement in the mortgage sector. This means completely privatising these government-sponsored enterprises, Fannie Mae and Freddie Mac. The problem is that these vehicles are basically a creation of the Congress and the same people who were involved with creating these instruments and with expanding them are now in charge of re-regulating that industry. So it does not make one very optimistic about the outcome.

The US government response to the financial crisis

So let me say some things about the US response to the fiscal crisis. Of course, there was a big mid-term election in November 2010, which moved part of government away from Democrat control and towards the Republicans – particularly in the House of Representatives and somewhat in the US Senate. I think part of what was going on in that period was that there was general opposition to a lot of what the government had done in response to the crisis. In particular there was opposition to a large amount of government expenditure in response to the recession, starting in 2008 while George W. Bush was still president and going into 2009.

Preventing financial institutions from failing

My view is not that all the spending in response to the crisis was wrong. I am not just uniformly opposed to everything that the government did in response to the financial crisis. Maybe it is not consistent with what Hayek would have thought but I draw a big distinction between the financial bailouts and the rest of the fiscal stimulus package and other interventions by the US government. If you go back to where the situation was in 2008, particularly when Lehman Brothers went bankrupt on 15 September 2008, I thought that we were in a really difficult situation that was threatening a Great Depression kind of outcome, as I described a little bit before. In that environment I think it was true that some major financial institutions were too big to fail, in the sense that the cost to the economy and the taxpayers was too much to accept. Because of that, I thought it was a better outcome to have the government intervene as necessary to prevent those kinds of collapses. That was the view of the government to some extent, except that it let Lehman go bankrupt in September of 2008, which I thought was a major mistake on the day it happened. Indeed, I think the US government decided about ten hours later, or whatever, that it was in fact a big error to allow that institution to go bankrupt! Overall I think the financial bailout part of the spending package, which is a bit less than a trillion dollars in terms of the amount of money the government contributed (much of this eventually recouped), was unfortunate but necessary and wise under the circumstances. The rest of the fiscal expansion I thought was mostly a waste of money. So I draw a big distinction between those two parts of the package, but I think that, within the US electorate, there was opposition to all of it.

After Lehman, of course, there were a number of other larger interventions, AIG being probably the most important. So, as I mentioned, after 15 September the US Treasury and the Federal Reserve changed their viewpoints and decided they could no longer afford a bankruptcy of the type that Lehman had undergone and therefore did everything they could to prevent further implosions of that type. These interventions ensured that AIG, Morgan Stanley, Citibank, etc. did not go under. I think that was the correct position. I think it is very unfortunate from a moral hazard standpoint but I think these institutions really were in a too-big-to-fail situation in terms of where we had gotten to at the end of 2008.

The fiscal stimulus package

So let me talk about the fiscal stimulus package. Hayek would probably be more appreciative of my views on this part of the government intervention. The US fiscal stimulus package in 2009/10 basically added up to something around $800 billion. This used to be a big number! I think this is mostly a waste of money. I do not think it has done a lot to retard the recession or to promote the economic recovery. I think the Obama administration is vastly overestimating the contribution of this package to US economic outcomes.

Some of this comes down to estimates of the so-called spending multiplier: that is of the effect on real gross domestic product of the government spending an extra dollar, particularly by increasing purchases of goods and services by a dollar. The government basically assumes that the spending multiplier is around two. Now, if that were correct, that would be another remarkable and magical thing, like the Alt-A mortgages and the sub-prime paper. If the multiplier is two it is quite amazing. It means that you can create something out of nothing just by spending another dollar. You not only get the dollar back, but you get another dollar. So even if the government is spending money on things that are totally wasteful – such as Keynes's example of digging holes and filling them up – it is nevertheless a good idea. So this is a remarkable vision about how the private economy operates, that somehow it is so inefficient that by doing this apparently foolish kind of intervention you end up making things better.

Now, I should say by way of confession that I used to be a Keynesian and I did a lot of work in macroeconomics on Keynesian models, but I kind of got over it and, in terms of economic theory and more particularly in terms of empirical evidence, I really don't think this is a good way of viewing how the macroeconomy operates. I have spent a lot of time on research recently trying to estimate the value of the spending multiplier and there is some other research that other people have been doing that I think is increasingly informative about the magnitude of the multiplier.

As a rough estimate, I think that the spending multiplier is small but positive in the short run, which means that GDP goes up but not by as much as the amount that the government is spending. So a multiplier of about a half I think is roughly reasonable in terms of a one-year response – a short-run type of response. Now, if you factor that into what the government did in 2009 and 2010, what you get is that the GDP growth rate in 2009 would have been higher by one percentage point than it would have been otherwise. So the spending has a positive contribution to GDP growth in the short term but not that big – much smaller than the administration has estimated. The effect on growth the next year is smaller because you have already kicked things up the first year and then you are trying to keep activity at that level. And then when you reduce the expenditure, because this is supposed to be a temporary programme to stimulate the economy, then of course the effect becomes negative. That is 2011 when you are reversing the stimulus programmes. The longer-run effect is much more negative because you have inflated the public debt by a very large amount, not only in the United States but also in the UK and elsewhere. And, ultimately, you have to pay for that not by fiscal deficits, not by borrowing, but by raising taxes of some form. When you raise the taxes you create a further negative effect on the economy because the taxes are distortionary and they tend to have negative incentive effects on investment and production.

Other people have estimated the effect on the economy of an increase in taxes, and, of course, in general, it depends on how you increase taxes. But the ultimate answer is that the effect is negative and larger in magnitude than the stimulus you got from the government expenditure. So I argue that the spending multiplier typically is around a half, the tax multiplier is clearly bigger than one in magnitude and has a negative sign. So, of course, if you put the two together you get a so-called 'balanced budget multiplier', which Keynes also talked about. And since the tax effect is larger, the balanced budget multiplier is negative, and that is the sort of medium- and longer-run effect from fiscal stimulus. It is clearly negative in terms of economic growth, and we are now moving into that part of this episode.

The bottom line here is that the only reason you might want to spend $800 billion on public sector programmes is if you think that those programmes are really productive from a social return perspective – in other words, we should not increase spending to create a stimulus but should use the sort of usual calculus that microeconomists would go through. So if you are thinking about building a highway you figure out something about the social rate of return and if it were high enough then maybe it is worth it. I think that is the right calculus and it should be used as much during the recession as at any other time. Of course, that is not the reasoning that went into the stimulus package in the USA and, I think, in many other countries.

So far, I have just mentioned the spending side of the Obama programme. There are also some items that are described as 'tax cuts'. But, in fact, until December of last year the tax cuts were not really tax rate cuts. They were not changes that gave people more incentives to do things such as invest. The tax cuts were basically throwing money at people, essentially a transfer payment and not a tax cut. The December 2010 tax agreement was a bit different. This was forced on President Obama by the November elections, and he agreed in that package to keep intact the tax rate structure that had been put in place under Bush in 2003, and they introduced a cut in the social security payroll tax. So I have mixed feelings about that aspect of the stimulus package. It is a cut in a marginal tax rate, unlike all the rest of the things that were done. But, on the other side, the social security payroll tax is actually the most efficient part of the revenue-raising scheme by the USA. So if you're going to cut tax rates it is probably not the favoured place to go: the social security payroll tax is way down the list of what would be an effective tax rate to cut. But at least it is a cut in a tax rate which is different from the other parts of the programme.

There is evidence, more detailed evidence than of course I can go through here, that cuts in marginal tax rates do have positive effects on economic growth. I don't mean to seem like an extreme 'supply-sider'. Such people sometimes express the view that you can cut tax rates and actually get more revenue, but I think it is definitely the case that, if you cut marginal tax rates, you get a response in terms of more economic activity, and I have some quantitative estimates of that. I think that worked, particularly in the 1980s under Reagan, and to a lesser extent under the programmes that the younger George Bush had, particularly in 2003.

There is a series of other programmes that the Obama administration put into place that I think has been unfortunate. I think the bailout of General Motors was a mistake. I think General Motors, unlike Lehman Brothers, could very easily have been allowed to go bankrupt and be bought out by some other private companies. I do not think that General Motors was too big to fail in the same sense that I think some major financial institutions are and, if we have time to talk about it, I can try to address why I think there is a difference there. The healthcare law, of course, is also a problem. The most curious intervention of the government, however, was the so-called 'cash for clunkers' programme. I don't know whether this programme is well publicised in the UK, but this is one of the most idiotic programmes ever designed by a government. It basically involved the government paying people to destroy functioning used cars and then give them a form of a credit to buy new cars. The consequence of that was that you destroyed some perfectly productive cars and, at the same time, you changed the timing of when people bought other automobiles. It did not do anything in terms of the longer-run investment in the purchase of cars. This programme, curiously enough, shows that incentives actually matter. The incentives here were all perverse, but people did respond to those incentives – it is not that people ignored them.

A more important mistake – and I find I get attacked viciously if I ever mention it – is that the government made the unemployment insurance programme much more generous than it used to be in the United States. We had a well-functioning programme of unemployment insurance. The basic idea was that the typical programme was 26 weeks in duration and during recessions the duration for which people were eligible for benefits was raised from 26 weeks to about twice that length. That is what had been done several times. And it makes sense on economic grounds that the duration should be longer when there is a general recession than at other times. But what happened in 2009 was that, all of a sudden, the eligibility was raised to 99 weeks, which is almost four times the normal duration. I think that this extension to the programme had incentive effects that raised the unemployment rate, made it more persistently high and, especially, made the duration of unemployment much higher than it has ever been in the United States. This change to the unemployment insurance programme has probably increased unemployment by one to two percentage points. This means that unemployment, which is now just over 9 per cent, could have been around 8 per cent or below. But I find that if I raise this point I am just described as not being a caring person because I don't want to give more money to the poor and, in particular, to the poor who are unemployed. So I find that it is very difficult to discuss this matter. Maybe here I can discuss it, but often it is difficult.

I think that it is also a problem for the United States that the Obama administration was preceded by the Bush administration, which was almost as bad. There was a tremendous expansion of government under Bush and it really reversed the achievements in the 1980s and the 1990s under Reagan and Clinton. I think of Reagan and Clinton as twins, but Obama and Bush are also kind of twins with respect to economic policy. There is a list of problematic policies arising from the Bush era which we do not seem to be able to get rid of. One of the craziest of these is the ethanol subsidy programme. This is not only idiotic like 'cash for clunkers' but is much bigger. The effects are also much more consequential. Basically we are burning up half of the corn crop in order to produce fuel inefficiently. So you see how hard it is to get rid of these government programmes once they are put into place.

The Federal Reserve response to the financial crash

Let me say something about monetary policy, which I think is equally applicable to the UK as to the USA, but I will talk about the Federal Reserve in the United States. One part of the monetary policy response to the financial crash and its aftermath was fairly conventional but very substantial in magnitude. This was the reduction in nominal interest rates – short-term interest rates – in response to a severe recession. I think that this was basically a reasonable policy. You can see the effect in Figure 7. This figure shows the Federal Funds rate, which has been zero, roughly speaking, for some time now, in response to the Great Recession. And I think that this was actually reasonable and I still think it is reasonable to keep the rates at the low level that they are currently at.

I don't know if I am going to discuss it now but this (2003–05) is the period that turned Greenspan from a hero into a villain. It used to be that Greenspan 'walked on water' and he could never

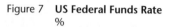

Figure 7   **US Federal Funds Rate**
%

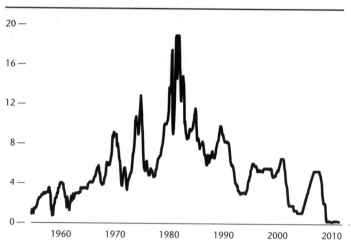

do or say anything that anybody from any political party really criticised. But the sharp reduction in interest rates in response to the mild recession of 2001/02 is very surprising. It is very surprising how sharply rates were cut at that time and those rate cuts are thought to be one of the factors underlying the housing boom which I looked at before. But I won't dwell on that at the moment.

The more surprising part of the Federal Reserve's response – the quantitative easing part – really explains how much the Fed's balance sheet has expanded. If you look at the Fed's balance sheet since early 2008, from before the crisis really hit, it expanded by $2 trillion, which is a big amount of money. US GDP is $15 trillion so, in relation to that, $2 trillion is an enormous sum. The Fed's balance sheet used to be less than $1 trillion, so this is a tremendous proportionate expansion. Initially, which I found even more surprising at the time, the Federal Reserve mainly expanded its balance sheet by buying up mortgage-backed securities. They accumulated more than $1 trillion worth of mortgage-backed securities. At that point the Federal Reserve didn't look all that different from the way Lehman Brothers looked in late 2008. It had all this short-term financing in effect and it was holding all these risky securities which are particularly linked into the housing market. I did not think this made any sense. It made the Federal Reserve look like a development bank. The Fed was intervening in particular sectors of the economy and this was really threatening central bank independence; it had a very risky portfolio. I did not really understand this kind of choice and I believe that the Bank of England did not do this kind of activity.

More recently, in the so-called QE2 phase, the Fed did something more traditional. They bought up US government securities – another $800 billion basically. They expanded the balance sheet, but this time buying treasury bonds rather than mortgage bonds. I don't think that there's much impact on the economy from the latest activity, and that would be equally true for the Bank of England as for the Federal Reserve. You have a situation where nominal short-term interest rates are essentially zero, and what the central bank is doing with these operations is taking on to its books longer-maturity securities. I don't know what the average maturity is of the bonds the central bank is buying, but let's say they are, on average, five-year bonds. In return the central bank is getting people to hold much shorter-term assets, such as reserves held on the books of the central bank, which pay slightly positive nominal interest rates but rates that are close to zero

– like US Treasury bills now. So what that accomplishes is that the private sector is holding shorter-term maturity instruments than it would have been otherwise: instead of holding five-year bonds it is holding overnight instruments. Well, firstly, I don't think that is going to matter very much; and, secondly, the US Treasury could have done that by itself without the central bank. If it wanted to fund the government by printing more treasury bills – by issuing very short-term paper – the US Treasury can do that. It does not need the central bank. So basically I don't think that quantitative easing is going to have very much impact.

There is a question about whether this vast liquidity expansion is inflationary. Normally economists have thought that, if you have this tremendous volume of open market operations – the purchase of debt by central banks – it would be inflationary. The reason it is not inflationary in the current environment is that people, or companies, are willing to hold vast amounts of short-term paper at close to zero nominal interest rates because people still think that the economy is very risky and they like paper that looks secure even if it pays very low interest rates. The Federal Reserve can increase reserves by, say, a trillion dollars and buy up a trillion dollars of treasury bonds. It is not inflationary because people are willing to just hold the trillion dollars of extra reserves. So as long as people are willing to do that, it does not have much effect on the real economy but it is also not inflationary, so it just doesn't matter that much.

A difficulty with the Fed's approach is that it compromises the so-called 'exit strategy'. In other words, if the economy eventually recovers and interest rates go up, then the Fed is going to have to reverse this whole process if it does not want quantitative easing to become inflationary. That is the so-called 'exit strategy'.

The usual way to do this would be to sell off the securities that the central bank has accumulated, whether it is mortgage securities or US government bonds. At the same time this would correspondingly reduce reserves of high-powered money. The problem with this approach is that it is supposed to be – or might be – contractionary, so there is a risk that the Fed will reignite a recession. On the other hand, if they do not sell back the securities they have bought, it is going to be inflationary. That is supposed to be the problem. I think Bernanke in the USA is too confident about how he can handle this. He is certainly well aware of this problem, but I think that he is too confident about being able to handle it. This could be a serious threat going forward.

On the other hand, I always think financial markets know more than I do and, if you look at US government bonds (both nominal bonds and inflation-linked bonds), there is no expectation of high inflation, even going out ten years in that market. Expected inflation is something like 2 per cent, maybe 2.5 per cent if you look over five years. So the financial markets seem to be confident that there won't be a lot of inflation. Now, that could be because nobody thinks there is ever going to be a recovery, or it could be because people think there is going to be a recovery and that the Fed will handle the exit strategy satisfactorily. The issues with regard to the Bank of England and its handling of the exit strategy from quantitative easing would be analogous.

The coming crisis – 'crises of governments'

I think the most likely source of the next crisis is what I call 'crises of governments'. There is a lot of fragility in this respect. A good deal of it has to do with the longer-term lack of fiscal discipline which has become more apparent recently, especially for some European governments, but also for US states. This is where these issues have become most clear.

Problems in the Eurozone

There is a serious threat, deriving from the lack of fiscal discipline, to the maintenance of the Eurozone as it has been constructed. This of course relates, in the first instance, to the crisis in Greece, Portugal and Ireland. It will be more serious if it spreads to Spain and Italy because they are much larger. If it does spread to Spain and Italy that will be a source of acute danger for the Eurozone. The euro should have been just a currency zone and I think that, as a common currency, it would have made a lot of sense.

When I spent a year in England in 1995 the big issue was whether the UK should join the euro – that was very contentious at the time. My view then was that a common currency would be a good idea for the UK. Unfortunately you could not join the common currency without getting a lot of other baggage, and the other baggage was that it was a semi-fiscal and political union. The UK did not want either of those things. In retrospect, of course, the UK is now very happy that it stayed out of this arrangement.

I do not understand the argument that people have some-times made that, if you are going to have a common currency, you have to have a fiscal union and maybe some kind of political union. I don't know any evidence that supports that position and conceptually it does not make sense to me. Another way to put it is this: if Greece wants to issue bonds denominated in euros, that should be fine, but it should not – and need not – be the business of the other countries and governments to prop up those bonds in terms of guaranteeing their repayment. That is the part of the development of the Eurozone that is troublesome. And, of course, if Greece is in a situation where Germany is going to bail it out all the time there is not enough incentive for fiscal discipline and it is the lack of that discipline that is the source of the crisis itself.

Fiscal problems in US states

There are a lot of parallels with the situation of some US states. Their problems are analogous to the problems in the Eurozone. The problem for US states is not so much that there is too much formal government borrowing financed by the issuing of government bonds. The problem relates to implicit promises – and sometimes explicit ones – that the state governments have made, particularly in terms of overly generous pension and healthcare benefits. For example, California and Illinois have enormous problems with unfunded defined-benefit pension liabilities and healthcare benefits.

This problem is what may bankrupt a lot of the US states ultimately. They have made promises that seem to be fiscally impossible to keep in many circumstances. Default on these obligations is more likely than default on government bonds. I do not know what is going to happen in the end. If Illinois decides, 'I was only kidding when I said you could have these pensions for ever and they are too big', what is the US government going to do in response to that? Is that kind of decision going to trigger some kind of default? Is the US government going to bail the states out? Is the US government going to say that state governments are too big to fail? Which, to repeat, I thought was true for Lehman but not for General Motors. So I am not sure how this is going to work out, but it is not so different from the problems with the euro.

The need for fiscal reform: curtailing expenditure

There is a need for some basic fiscal reforms. This should not be a controversial statement. A lot of this should be in terms of curtailing government expenditures. You have to keep in mind that there was a vast expansion in the USA of various government programmes, both under Bush and Obama, so part of this process is just getting back to where we were in 2000. But then there is also this longer-term structural problem related to the major entitlement programmes and the promises that have already been made – particularly social security pensions and the medical programmes. These form a major burden which would have been there even in the absence of the financial crisis. As such, fundamental fiscal reform has to feature sharp curtailing of spending, particularly of the major entitlement programmes such as Social Security, Medicare and Medicaid.

The need for tax reform

Some major tax reforms also need to be part of this package. So, for example, I would get rid of the corporate income tax in the United States. That form of taxation makes no sense and it does not raise very much money. I would not have an inheritance tax. You could also raise revenues by cutting back on so-called tax expenditure items which are deductions from income tax for certain forms of expenditure such as mortgage interest, state and local taxes and employee fringe benefits. But the bigger question in the USA is whether to have a value added tax or generalised sales tax, which is one of the favourite taxes in western Europe.

The value added tax is a very efficient form of taxation which is both the plus and the minus of the system. More or less like the payroll tax in the USA, the value added tax is very good at generating a lot of revenue and it causes fewer distortions for a given amount of revenue raised. On the other hand this is bad because when government has available this kind of money machine it tends to grow larger and spend more! That is the key trade-off in terms of efficient taxation, and whether you want it or not. But in the USA I do not really see an alternative because I think that, given the status of the entitlement programmes and where they are going, the USA will have to have more revenue. I do not see an alternative to a VAT form of taxation. So I think a value added tax is coming at some point. Larry Summers had a famous statement here about why we do not have a value added tax in the United States. He said that it was because the Democrats thought it was regressive and the Republicans thought it was a money machine, and a sort of political equilibrium between those two forces prevented it being enacted. Then he followed the statement up by saying 'we are going to have a value added tax in the US when the Democrats realise that it's a money machine and the Republicans realise that it's regressive'. There are pluses and minuses of the value added tax, but I think it is coming. In fact, I think the USA is the only OECD country that actually does not have this system.

A double-dip recession?

I want to finish by talking about the chance of a double-dip recession. Things looked a little better six months ago or so, and I think

Obama made his best economic intervention in December 2010 by preserving the tax rate structure and for about a week not saying that you had to tax the rich at a higher rate because they are bad people! He actually did have a tax rate cut as part of the package as I have already mentioned.

But there are various indicators that look quite weak with respect to the recovery in the USA. These include GDP growth; the outlook for the labour market – particularly with regard to the sustained high unemployment rate; the outlook for house prices, which really are not recovering; the stock market, which, having done pretty well for a while, then turned downwards; and the underlying fiscal issues that have not yet been seriously dealt with. You do hear some voices in the USA that I think are more rational than usual, but it is not clear at this point how things are going to work out in terms of solving the basic fiscal problems that we have. There are also these questions about future inflation which I have already discussed a bit. Again, the financial markets seem to be quite optimistic in that regard. And then there is the broader question about the potential default on some government obligations, which is part of this 'crisis of governments' that I have outlined. This problem is somewhat more acute in Europe and it is a little hard to see how Europe is going to escape from the crisis, but, to repeat, the US states are another great source of concern. So, on balance, I do not end up being terribly optimistic at this stage and I am sorry to have to end on this note.

2 QUESTIONS AND DISCUSSION

QUENTIN LANGLEY: If banks are too big to fail, should they be broken up? And, if so, now or later?

ROBERT BARRO: I think this is part of the more general question about what kind of regulatory changes you would want that particularly relate to financial institutions. One consequence of the crisis has been a tremendous outpouring of research on that question in terms of why did you have this financial implosion. What kind of regulations seem to improve matters? I think some of the capital requirements coming out of the Bank for International Settlements are sensible in terms of basically increasing the capital requirements. And sometimes it is proposed to do that in a progressive manner, which is discouraging financial institutions from growing too large. It is puzzling about the too-big-to-fail thing. Because on the one hand, you get these institutions that seem to have that status, and then the government feels, I think accurately, that it has to bail them out *ex post*. But, on the other hand, if you look at what the government relies on, in terms of solving some of these problems at least temporarily, it relies on very large institutions: for example, JPMorgan taking over Bear Stearns or something analogous to that. So I think there are regulatory changes that have been proposed that could make the system work more effectively. Whether one predicts that governments will actually move in a direction where, on average, the changes in regulations are favourable is a different matter. I would not be too optimistic about that because they are probably more likely to make changes that will make things worse rather than better.

RUPERT FAST: If injecting more money into the economy through quantitative easing doesn't cause inflation, what do you make of the rampant inflation people are experiencing in the UK, when incomes are barely rising at all? And is there a risk that this will turn us into a Second World country?

ROBERT BARRO: I start from the proposition that if you just told me that the Federal Reserve in the United States had suddenly expanded high-powered money by $2 trillion, then I would have said that this would be very inflationary. That would be the normal kind of response. However, in the USA, for example, the inflation rate has ticked up a little bit, but not that much.

SPEAKER: Rubbish.

ROBERT BARRO: I don't know why you say rubbish. You think the statistics are unreliable?

There have been other developments in the world, related to commodity prices, and related to food prices. And indeed, the ethanol programme is part of the rationale for why food prices have increased so much. So some prices, of course, have gone up. But I don't really have a problem in believing that the overall index of prices, for example the Consumer Price Index in the United States, is reasonably reliable. And you've seen a bit of an uptick in inflation, but not very much. And as I mentioned, in terms of expectations in the financial markets, expectations of future inflation are relatively low. That is also true in the UK. So my belief is that there has been a temporary blip in inflation, related to certain prices rising, but not that it is an endemic thing. So you put that along with the quantitative easing, and you would have thought that quantitative easing would be inflationary. So in the lecture I was trying to interpret why I thought it had not been more inflationary than it has been. But, again, it is important to stress that the nature of the exit strategy is crucial, in terms of the longer-term implications.

MATTHEW SINCLAIR: To what extent do you think China is likely to continue to perform strongly, or is it likely to suffer a hard landing as a result of what appears to be an asset boom there?

ROBERT BARRO: Overall, I'm optimistic about the China experiment, which really goes back to roughly 1979, when they decided to become a market economy to some extent, relative to the previous system. There is a lot of potential there for further convergence towards the richer states in the world. Today, they have only about one seventh of the per capita GDP of the USA. So, even though they have been growing for more than twenty years – indeed, almost thirty years – at quite a high rate, there is still quite a bit of potential, in terms of this convergence. There are a number of potential pitfalls for China, which I have thought about for some time. I think there are two major pitfalls. First, on the political side there is the problem of what will be the nature of the political liberalisation, which usually has to come when countries get more prosperous. How are they going to move towards something that looks more like democracy with more civil liberties? Is that transition going to involve some kind of violence, which it could have done in 1989, but of course there was a different outcome at that point? Secondly, there is this tremendous rural/urban divide. So a lot of the growth has been focused in the urban areas, and that produces a lot of other tensions, related to internal mobility. I would have focused on those factors, rather than on the asset boom or the big infrastructure investment boom that the Chinese government has initiated. I have less concern about that, than about these other two points that I mentioned.

LINDA WHETSTONE: You ended up on a pessimistic note. You obviously know a huge amount about these things. But you didn't make suggestions. For instance, what should the US and UK governments be doing to make the economic outlook more optimistic in a year or two's time?

ROBERT BARRO: Well, if I go back to 2009, in the USA, for example, I think it is quite appropriate to have a fiscal deficit in response to a large recession. I would have focused all the response on the tax side. I would not have been doing a lot of expenditure programmes, that don't seem to have any rationale intrinsically because they are not really productive public sector activities. So, I would have focused it all on the tax side. And on the tax side, I would have focused on things that have incentive effects. This means that you want to cut tax rates, not just throw money at people. So I think I could be able to come up with a pretty good concrete programme for what such a tax reform package would have looked like. And I would still want to go forward in that direction, so I would not be following the expenditure programmes. As I mentioned, I thought a lot of the financial sector bailouts were unavoidable. And I wasn't really criticising that part of the response which occurred, starting in 2008, going into 2009.

FEMALE SPEAKER: I hope Keynes did not use Germany for his general theory in 1936. Not everyone, even today, knows that Germany had the money to reflate her economy in 1933. She was the world's greatest exporter in 1931, in terms of value. She also had 40 per cent cover for her banknotes in the Reichsbank. She used deflation for political ends in the Great Depression. Germany is not the same country as she was then, but can we reflate our economy when she is still in deflationary mode – indeed, when Europe is in deflationary mode?

ROBERT BARRO: So you know, I have done this study of rare macroeconomic disaster events using lots of countries and data over a period that is longer than a hundred years. So Germany is an interesting case there, because they experienced all the bad events between the two world wars. They had four macro disaster events in the period between 1913 and 1948, including the two world wars, but also the depression. It had its own hyperinflation, which was associated with the aftermath from World War One. So Germany has been quite an interesting case, from that perspective. Keynes actually started doing work that was maybe more serious, which was about hyperinflation and about government revenue from printing money. And a lot of that was applicable to the extreme inflation period of Germany. I think it is true that, after the hyperinflation, Germany was more sensitive to that issue than most other countries. And that is why Germany would have a tendency towards deflation, and also towards price stability, which I think is a characteristic that is still there. People think that this has to do with the history of the hyperinflation in the early 1920s; I am not sure how correct that is.

NIGEL VINSON: Can I come back to the issue of infrastructure development? The infrastructure in this country is almost Third World. People come here to go potholing on our roads. Wouldn't it be sensible to put contra-cyclical finance into our declining infrastructure, where it undoubtedly would yield economic benefits? And would it also have a much higher multiplier effect, probably even up to two or three, if this were done?

ROBERT BARRO: I'm not basically an anarchist. I don't think that there is nothing governments can do that is useful. And filling potholes is probably one of the most useful activities that governments undertake, and it's always a shame they don't do more of it – I certainly see that in my own locality. So, I am not disputing the idea that there might be useful social investments of that type. It would be a matter of looking at the particulars, if you are talking about a particular airport, particular highway and so on. And I am not saying that those are bad ideas in general. However, I don't think they become so much better ideas during a time of recession than they are at other times. It is a question of getting the social rate of return that makes it worthwhile putting the resources into those activities. Otherwise, if you are just trying to expand the economy because you think there is a downturn, as I mentioned, I think you should focus your efforts on the tax side and particularly on tax rates. So I don't regard recession as a justification for public expenditures that are not worthwhile in terms of the social rate of return per se. But that does not exclude airports and highways: I just don't know if you particularly want to build these things in bad economic times. Japan is the real example of this. Japan used to be a low public debt economy. And they have had a vast expansion of public sector borrowing. And a lot of it has been to finance all sorts of infrastructure activities. It never really helped in terms of the economic growth of Japan, which has been quite weak for some time. But interestingly, every time they did it, every time they had some kind of infrastructure investment boom, and it didn't seem to help economic growth, the response from some economists was that they just did not do enough! And that is the same with the US fiscal stimulus package. We did this programme, which was around $800 billion, and the results look disappointing. I think everybody agrees they look disappointing. I take that as some indication that maybe we should not have followed the programme. But the response from a lot of Keynesian economists is that Obama did not do enough. My great friend Paul Krugman always has that viewpoint, for example. He argues that we just didn't go far enough; we didn't stick with it long enough. But then you never seem to get the answer, from supporters of such programmes, 'well, maybe this wasn't such a good device for curing a recession, in terms of governments expanding their expenditure on various activities'. Of course, it is also true, and I don't think that this is really controversial, that most of the fiscal stimulus stuff in the USA was not on these kinds of social expenditures that you are suggesting are productive. That really is not what it was composed of. And somebody gave me this good line yesterday saying it was basically shovel-ready stuff. But anything that's shovel-ready must not be very productive, in terms of social rates of return. There must be something funny about it, if they can all of a sudden spend all this money in a quick way. It must mean that it's not really a high rate of return from a social perspective.

MICHAEL LYON: I am afraid the gentleman just asked more or less the question I had in mind. But perhaps I could just develop it slightly, which is to say that I think what perhaps is being groped for is a smarter approach to government expenditure in terms of the fiscal response, rather than the somewhat crude response that we're taught from Keynes, and the holes in the roads examples. Do you think that there might be scope for economists to develop their thinking on that? For example, it would require things such as medium-term tax-balance criteria on the selection of investment projects and so forth.

ROBERT BARRO: So the problem is that, if you really think the spending multiplier is around two, which, for example, is the view to which the US government subscribes, then you basically just want to do a lot of it. It is better to do something productive than non-productive, but it's not that critical. So I think understanding the value of the multiplier – at least approximately – is central to thinking about this kind of fiscal response on the expenditure side. The US government really believes that their multiplier is something like two and I think that explains a lot of the nature of the response. On the tax side, I think there are a lot of good proposals for how you can make the tax system more productive, particularly in the United States, and I think a lot of that makes sense. And I think there are some good reforms that could be made there, that would promote economic growth over the medium term and longer term.

GRAEME LEACH: In what circumstances can you achieve an expansionary fiscal contraction? How do you get a negative multiplier?

ROBERT BARRO: I take that question seriously and I have been trying in my own research agenda – and also there is other people's research – to try to get a better idea on exactly that kind of issue. For example, think about transfer payments. Is it right that, when the government borrows more money and gives it to people, maybe unemployed people, it has a positive effect on GDP? Is that expansionary? I don't know any empirical evidence on that question. But a lot of macroeconomists believe that it is true. Therefore they believe the reverse, that when you have the contraction in welfare benefits, it is going to be contractionary for the economy. But I repeat, I don't know any empirical evidence on that question. There is accumulated sub-evidence about the response of the economy when the government is doing more activities that look like purchases of goods and services: it is from there that I got the spending multiplier of around a half, which came from some particular kinds of evidence, which we could debate. But at least it came from somewhere. I understand some of the magnitudes involving tax changes and the response of the economy, but in terms of some of these other magnitudes, people argue as if they know the answers to these things and I think that they are just taking their answers from basically nowhere. So it would be a good product from this current, global Great Recession if, as I think was suggested some time before, you had the data from all these different responses from different countries, some with more contractionary policies, and some with more extravagant expansions. And then we could look at what was the answer to that question about 'expansionary fiscal contractions'.

Now, from an economist's point of view, what you really want is a situation where the governments are following different policies randomly. That is, randomly you say, 'Well, OK, Germany, you have to be conscientious and tough; Greece, you do the opposite.' You want the assignment to be unrelated to the economic structure. The problem is that this is not exactly the way the data come. But maybe somebody could be clever enough to use the results of this episode – 2008 to 2011 or so – and evaluate the different responses to give us better answers to some of those questions, not all of which I think I have the answers to.

ABOUT THE IEA

The Institute is a research and educational charity (No. CC 235 351), limited by guarantee. Its mission is to improve understanding of the fundamental institutions of a free society by analysing and expounding the role of markets in solving economic and social problems.

The IEA achieves its mission by:

- a high-quality publishing programme
- conferences, seminars, lectures and other events
- outreach to school and college students
- brokering media introductions and appearances

The IEA, which was established in 1955 by the late Sir Antony Fisher, is an educational charity, not a political organisation. It is independent of any political party or group and does not carry on activities intended to affect support for any political party or candidate in any election or referendum, or at any other time. It is financed by sales of publications, conference fees and voluntary donations.

In addition to its main series of publications the IEA also publishes a termly journal, *Economic Affairs*.

The IEA is aided in its work by a distinguished international Academic Advisory Council and an eminent panel of Honorary Fellows. Together with other academics, they review prospective IEA publications, their comments being passed on anonymously to authors. All IEA papers are therefore subject to the same rigorous independent refereeing process as used by leading academic journals.

IEA publications enjoy widespread classroom use and course adoptions in schools and universities. They are also sold throughout the world and often translated/reprinted.

Since 1974 the IEA has helped to create a worldwide network of 100 similar institutions in over 70 countries. They are all independent but share the IEA's mission.

Views expressed in the IEA's publications are those of the authors, not those of the Institute (which has no corporate view), its Managing Trustees, Academic Advisory Council members or senior staff.

Members of the Institute's Academic Advisory Council, Honorary Fellows, Trustees and Staff are listed on the following page.

The Institute gratefully acknowledges financial support for its publications programme and other work from a generous benefaction by the late Alec and Beryl Warren.

The Institute of Economic Affairs
2 Lord North Street, Westminster, London SW1P 3LB
Tel: 020 7799 8900
Fax: 020 7799 2137
Email: iea@iea.org.uk
Internet: iea.org.uk

Other papers recently published by the IEA include:

The Legal Foundations of Free Markets
Edited by Stephen F. Copp
Hobart Paperback 36; ISBN 978 0 255 36591 8; £15.00

Climate Change Policy: Challenging the Activists
Edited by Colin Robinson
Readings 62; ISBN 978 0 255 36595 6; £10.00

Should We Mind the Gap?
Gender Pay Differentials and Public Policy
J. R. Shackleton
Hobart Paper 164; ISBN 978 0 255 36604 5; £10.00

Pension Provision: Government Failure Around the World
Edited by Philip Booth et al.
Readings 63; ISBN 978 0 255 36602 1; £15.00

New Europe's Old Regions
Piotr Zientara
Hobart Paper 165; ISBN 978 0 255 36617 5; £12.50

Central Banking in a Free Society
Tim Congdon
Hobart Paper 166; ISBN 978 0 255 36623 6; £12.50

Verdict on the Crash: Causes and Policy Implications
Edited by Philip Booth
Hobart Paperback 37; ISBN 978 0 255 36635 9; £12.50

The European Institutions as an Interest Group
The Dynamics of Ever-Closer Union
Roland Vaubel
Hobart Paper 167; ISBN 978 0 255 36634 2; £10.00

An Adult Approach to Education
Alison Wolf
Hobart Paper 168; ISBN 978 0 255 36586 4; £10.00

Taxation and Red Tape
The Cost to British Business of Complying with the UK Tax System
Francis Chittenden, Hilary Foster & Brian Sloan
Research Monograph 64; ISBN 978 0 255 36612 0; £12.50

Ludwig von Mises – A Primer
Eamonn Butler
Occasional Paper 143; ISBN 978 0 255 36629 8; £7.50

Does Britain Need a Financial Regulator?
Statutory Regulation, Private Regulation and Financial Markets
Terry Arthur & Philip Booth
Hobart Paper 169; ISBN 978 0 255 36593 2; £12.50

Hayek's *The Constitution of Liberty*
An Account of Its Argument
Eugene F. Miller
Occasional Paper 144; ISBN 978 0 255 36637 3; £12.50

Fair Trade Without the Froth
A Dispassionate Economic Analysis of 'Fair Trade'
Sushil Mohan
Hobart Paper 170; ISBN 978 0 255 36645 8; £10.00

A New Understanding of Poverty
Poverty Measurement and Policy Implications
Kristian Niemietz
Research Monograph 65; ISBN 978 0 255 36638 0; £12.50

The Challenge of Immigration
A Radical Solution
Gary S. Becker
Occasional Paper 145; ISBN 978 0 255 36613 7; £7.50

Sharper Axes, Lower Taxes
Big Steps to a Smaller State
Edited by Philip Booth
Hobart Paperback 38; ISBN 978 0 255 36648 9; £12.50

Self-employment, Small Firms and Enterprise
Peter Urwin
Research Monograph 66; ISBN 978 0 255 36610 6; £12.50

Other IEA publications

Comprehensive information on other publications and the wider work of the IEA can be found at www.iea.org.uk. To order any publication please see below.

Personal customers

Orders from personal customers should be directed to the IEA:
Clare Rusbridge
IEA
2 Lord North Street
FREEPOST LON10168
London SW1P 3YZ
Tel: 020 7799 8907. Fax: 020 7799 2137
Email: crusbridge@iea.org.uk

Trade customers

All orders from the book trade should be directed to the IEA's distributor:
Gazelle Book Services Ltd (IEA Orders)
FREEPOST RLYS-EAHU-YSCZ
White Cross Mills
Hightown
Lancaster LA1 4XS
Tel: 01524 68765. Fax: 01524 53232
Email: sales@gazellebooks.co.uk

IEA subscriptions

The IEA also offers a subscription service to its publications. For a single annual payment (currently £42.00 in the UK), subscribers receive every monograph the IEA publishes. For more information please contact:
Clare Rusbridge
Subscriptions
IEA
2 Lord North Street
FREEPOST LON10168
London SW1P 3YZ
Tel: 020 7799 8907. Fax: 020 7799 2137
Email: crusbridge@iea.org.uk